My Life, My Struggles, My Story

A Transformational Journey from a Life of Childhood Abuse to a Life of Love, Joy, and Success

By Nelda Barba

Published by Social Buzz for Biz Publishing
1169 N Burleson Blvd. Suite 117
Burleson, Texas 76028
http://socialbuzzforbizpublishing.com

Printed in the United States of America

ISBN - 13: 978-0998613505
ISBN - 10: 0998613509

Publisher: Susan Ordona of Social Buzz for Biz Publishing
Cover Design by Jenn Foster and Rory Carruthers
Front Cover Photography by Alisia Thompson Photography
Edited by Carly Carruthers

Dedication

This book is dedicated

...to my three wonderful children and their families

...to my dearest grandson

...to my life partner, Richard Crawford

Thank you for always being there for me, for all the encouragement to always reach for the stars, and most of all, for giving me unconditional love endlessly.

This book is also dedicated to anyone who has suffered abuse.

Know that there is hope, and it doesn't have to define who you are.

Table of Contents

Foreword

Nelda Barba is a survivor. Her story is a universal one. It is the story of surviving abuse and the heartbreak that the betrayal implies. She is the archetype of the ordinary woman who has found her power through struggle and triumph over her difficult life experiences. Her journey continues, but her story is what makes her who she is today.

The Nelda Barba that I know is a dichotomy. She is tough, strong smart, and resilient. But more importantly, she has survived with an open heart. She is loving and giving to her family, students, and community. She is a wonderful mother, wife, teacher, and friend. There were paths that Nelda could have taken, but she chose to follow her heart, and that changed everything.

Nelda's journey from a difficult childhood in the Philippines to a gifted healer in Florida is difficult to read. But the lessons to be gleaned from her mistakes and triumphs are powerfully human. Her story will provide fuel for others struggling along their own similar paths. It is a story of hope. Nelda provides a role model for a person who refuses to be a victim to life's circumstances. Nelda and others like her, who have the courage to tell their stories, are touchstones to guide us along our own difficult paths. I want to thank Nelda for having the courage to tell her heartbreaking, but ultimately triumphant story.

- *Kitty Ramey,*
  Teacher, Media Specialist, and Guidance Counselor,
  B.S., M.Ed.

Introduction

I've never had a normal life.

When I was six years old, my life was turned upside down by my family. I endured many traumatic experiences as a child. The family that I loved and trusted betrayed me and abused me. Growing up, I remember asking God why I was being treated so horribly. Although I will never know why my family withheld their love, I always kept my faith in God and humanity.

My story is filled with many terrible and upsetting memories; however, it is also filled with kindness, strength, and perseverance. It is filled with new beginnings, passion, joy, and love.

I will never forget where I came from, but now I only look forward in this journey. I have so much to look forward to. My days are now filled with love and support as I help others at my yoga studio and cherish time with my family. I hope to continue to love and support others by sharing my story.

It has been difficult to revisit the darkest moments of my journey, but I know that I can be a voice out there for anyone who has gone through similar experiences. I am sharing my story to help others recognize that survivors of abuse can overcome, can find hope, can thrive and flourish. I hope you'll be strong enough to face your life's challenges and find peace and prosperity on your journey.

CHAPTER 1

The Night that Changed My Life

"There are wounds that never show on the body that are deeper and more hurtful than anything that bleeds."
- Laurell K. Hamilton

I was born into struggle, but have always had hope in my heart. My father passed away before I was born. My mother struggled to raise and provide for her three children while living in the slums of Tondo, Manila. Tondo is one of the most impoverished and underdeveloped areas in the Philippines. Although life was difficult, I felt loved and supported by my family. I remember fun times like going to the beach on the weekends with my mother. However, it wasn't meant to last.

When I was six years old, my family moved from my childhood home in Tondo, Manila to Olongapo City. My mother moved us in search of a better life. This was a huge change for me and my family. When I was growing up, there was a U.S. naval base in Olongapo City, and this brought more opportunities for work in the nightlife industry that catered to the military personnel stationed there. My mother had no education, so work was limited to the nightclubs and bars for the sailors.

My mother, brothers, and I moved into a five bedroom house where my godmother lived and was the landlord. My brother David was fourteen years old, and Jared was seventeen years old. All four of us lived in one of the bedrooms. We shared the kitchen and the bathroom with all the occupants of the other four bedrooms. Little did I know that the house was actually a brothel. At that time, I was too young to realize where we were.

*　*　*

My mother enrolled us in the nearby Tapinac Elementary School. School was difficult. The children made fun of me. My clothes were ugly. I felt ugly. I didn't have a school bag like the regular kids in school. All I had was a paper bag for my school books. I also struggled to learn and felt like I was always behind the rest of the class.

David was always the smart one, while Jared had a learning disability. Even though Jared couldn't read or write, the school started him in the fourth grade, since he was already seventeen years old. Soon after that, Jared quit school, moved away, and went to work as a mason somewhere in Gordon Heights, about 30 minutes from Olongapo City.

With Jared gone, it left just David, my mother, and me living in that small bedroom. My mother had the bed, while David and I slept on the floor.

My mother got a job as a hostess in a nightclub. She would leave the house around eight o'clock at night. During the day, she worked as a laundry woman for her boss, who owned the nightclub.

While my mother was at work, my brother David would watch over me. Although he was given the task of caretaker, David never really cared about me. Both of my brothers were never nice to me; they never treated me like I was their little sister.

* * *

One night, my life changed forever…

The nightmare began when I was in first grade. As my mother left for work, she reminded David to watch over me like big brothers do. However, he didn't listen.

When my mother was gone, my brother David did the unthinkable; he raped me!

While I was sleeping, he covered my mouth and pinned me down so I couldn't fight back. After this horrendous act, he said to me, "You better not say anything to anyone about what I did to you. No one is going to believe you anyway, you're just a child." Then he just went back to sleep.

All I could do was cry and cry and cry. I felt so dirty after being touched by my brother. I went back to sleep, all curled up in a little ball in the corner. I wanted to kill him for what he did to me. I cringe even now while writing about it. As I mention his name, I remember seeing his ugly face over me as he ruined my childhood.

* * *

The next morning, as I was getting ready for school, David couldn't look at me. He didn't even walk to school with me, so I had to walk by myself, while he walked with his friend, Eddie. It was very hard for me to deal with my difficult classmates. I remained silent and tried hard to focus on school, instead of thinking about the horrible events from the night before.

From that night on, I cursed him. I hated him so much for what he did to me. I couldn't believe that a brother could do that to his own sister. I was so upset and filled with anger, but I also believed him when he told me not to tell anyone.

My mother had no idea what happened. I became distant from my brother. I couldn't even look at him or talk to him. When my mother would ask why I wasn't talking to my brother, I would just say, "I don't want to."

David left me alone for a few weeks. As a precaution, I slept as far away from him as I could on the floor. I bundled myself with layers of clothes, trying to protect myself just in case he tried to do it again.

I felt so alone and betrayed. All I had to protect myself were my clothes. There was nobody I could turn to. In a single night, my childhood was ruined and life with my family would only get worse.

CHAPTER 2

A Loveless Family

"Childhood should be carefree, playing in the sun;
not living a nightmare in the darkness of the soul."

- Dave Pelzer, *A Child Called It*

One night when I came home, David was already sound asleep. As I'd been doing, I kept my street clothes on and bundled myself up, trying to protect myself, just in case. My mother came home with an American guy and brought him into our tiny room. I pretended to be sound asleep and had my back turned against them. They were talking in English, which I didn't understand. I just had to close my eyes tight. I don't know what time the guy left, but he was gone the next morning.

Over the next few weeks, my mother would bring different guys to our room every night. I never questioned her about why there were guys into our room. I guess David was old enough to know what kind of job our mother did for a living. I later found out that she had started bringing men into our room a few weeks after we moved into the house. I believe this is how David got the idea of raping me.

*   *   *

As soon as my mother left for work at night, I stayed out of the house for as long as possible. I wanted to avoid being alone in the same room with David. I would walk around nearby Magsaysay Avenue, which was a busy street with lots of activity. At an early age, I learned to sell chewing gum to American sailors on the street and made a little money. I thought David didn't know what I was doing because he was always busy playing outside with Eddie.

Unfortunately, David found out that I was selling chewing gum to make some money, and he told our mother. That didn't sit well with my mom. She was mad and beat me up with a belt that left marks on my bare skin all over my body. She said to me, "You are not to go out of this house when I go to work."

David laughed while I was beaten up by my mother. Then he left, played with his friends outside of the house, and later on, spent the night over at his friend Eddie's house across the street.

Meanwhile, my mom was getting ready for work. Before she left, she brought this portable potty from by the bathroom into our tiny bedroom. I asked her what it was for. "That's for you, so you can go to the bathroom here in the room, while I lock you in. You are to stay inside while I'm gone."

I started crying and begged her not to lock me up. I promised her I would not go out at night to sell chewing gum on the street ever again. I tugged on her dress, but she pushed me down on the floor. Then she was gone.

I stood there holding onto the strong bars of our window, crying, and feeling like I was in jail. I watched the neighborhood kids, including my brother, play. My godmother's nephew saw me behind our window bars looking out at all the children playing. He asked why I wasn't outside playing with all the other kids. All I could tell him was that I was serving my punishment for what I did.

The next day, my godmother confronted my mom. I could hear my mom telling her to mind her own business. My mom thought I was the one who told my godmother about being locked up, so she hit me again; this time harder than the previous time.

* * *

I went to school the next day. The other children continued to make fun of me. Although I was only in first grade, it had already come to a point where I did not care anymore about what those kids thought of me. It didn't matter.

From school, I'd come home to household chores that my mom already had in store for me.

Scrubbing and waxing the floor was the norm. Mom didn't want me to have friends. I never knew why, but I thought it was because I was a bad little girl.

As she was getting ready for work one evening, she told me that I was not going to be locked up anymore, but warned me not to leave the house. Of course, David was to report to her if I ever violated that. She made sure to tell me that if I did leave, she would hit me again. So, I listened and didn't leave the room again.

* * *

One night, my mom came home early from work. She said she wasn't busy at the nightclub.

David and I were already fast asleep, the farthest distance from each other in that tiny bedroom. My mom woke me up and said to get dressed as we were going to buy hot pandesal at the local bakery.

I was so happy. My mom was taking me to the bakery! I quickly got dressed, and soon we were walking down the street towards the bakery. Pandesal are delicious Filipino bread rolls that are usually enjoyed at night, hot and fresh from the oven. This was a real treat!

After getting our pandesal, my mother told me to stay right there at the store; she would come back for me. I dutifully said, "Ok, Mama." I don't know how long I stood there waiting for my mom. The next thing I noticed was that everybody on the street was running, walking fast, hurrying to go home so as not to break the curfew at midnight. In 1967, no one was supposed to be out on the street by that time.

Realizing that I had to get out of there, I started walking around, crying, and panicking since my mother never came back for me. I only knew one street to find my way home. As I was walking in the dark alley, I remembered a sign, something that reminded me of familiar sights. I continued walking for about ten minutes.

Eventually, I found our home. I couldn't tell the address since it was so dark. There were no street lights. I started wiggling the gate of the front of the house. It was locked every night by my godmother to deter burglars.

My godmother heard the noise of my wiggling her house gate, came down, and saw me standing by the gate. She asked me what I was doing there in the middle of the night. I told her what happened, that my mom left me downtown and never came back for me, so I had to find my way home.

Next thing I knew, my godmother was knocking on our bedroom door. When my mom opened the door, she saw me hiding behind my godmother. After my godmother confronted her about leaving me downtown, my mom grabbed me and shut the door. She told me to shut up and go to sleep.

At that moment, I felt my mom didn't want me back or even love me. I felt that she only loved David because he was smart and could read and write. I felt like I was just a burden to her.

* * *

Once the school year was over, my mom packed my bag and sent me to live with an old lady I'd never met before. She dropped me off with the premise of picking me up in a couple of months. She told the old lady that she couldn't take care of me, so she was paying her to care for me.

After my mom gave some money to the old lady, she went on her way. Without giving me a hug or a kiss goodbye, she was gone. I remember watching from the window as she disappeared from my sight...I was crying and crying.

Three weeks later, my mom came back. I was so excited since I thought she was there to pick me up. Instead, she just brought me a box of crackers and gave some money to the old lady.

Then she was gone again. This time, I didn't cry for her. I just continued to play with my dolls.

During the time I was in the care of the old lady, I never learned her name. Even though she wasn't nice to me, I felt safe. I was away from David.

Second grade was starting again soon, so my mom came to pick me up. She was very cold towards me. She didn't even give me a hug or a kiss.

* * *

One night when my mom left for work and I was already asleep, the nightmare happened again!

As David was running his filthy hands over me, I fought back. He hit me and pinned me down again with one hand on both of my arms and the other covering my mouth so I couldn't scream.

I have never felt so dirty in my life! I can't forget his words, "You better not tell anyone about this, do you hear me?"

I didn't even look at him. I wanted so badly to just get a knife and stab him to death, but I was so weak; I was just a helpless child! I prayed to God to just take me!

*   *   *

The next day, I went to school. I wanted to tell someone what happened to me, but I was in too much fear of David and my mom.

I became bitter towards them and bitter towards other kids. I never had any friends that I could talk to. I distanced myself from everyone.

I started asking myself, "Why? Why are they doing this to me. Doesn't God see what's happening to me? Why can't HE do something about it?"

I was only seven years old. My life was a mess. I'd been raped twice by my brother and beaten by my mom. I wondered, "What else is there in my life that's waiting for me?"

CHAPTER 3

The Struggle Continues

"Carve a tunnel of hope through a dark mountain of disappointment."

- Martin Luther King Jr.

David never touched me again. He finally graduated from elementary school. My mom was so proud of him and wanted him to continue to high school. Instead, David moved away. I didn't know where, but I didn't really care as long as he didn't come back.

During third grade, my mom and I moved away from Olongapo City to Gordon Heights. Mom rented a tiny little house with no indoor bathroom.

Out of nowhere, David showed up and stayed with us. Soon Jared found out that we were in Gordon Heights, so he moved in as well. There were four of us living in this tiny little house without a bathroom. To go to the bathroom, we had to go outside of the house. We had to bury our poop in the dirt.

* * *

Mom stopped working at the nightclub's bar. She was just working for her boss, Mr. Wong, washing clothes for his family. Sometimes when I saw her washing people's clothes for a living, it broke my heart because she had no trade or any other experience. When I saw her struggling just to make ends meet from day to day, I said to myself, "I don't want to end up like my mother." I am blessed everyday of my life knowing I didn't end up like her. There's a phrase, "Like mother, like daughter." Thankfully, I didn't end up like my mother. I believe that watching her struggle in life taught me the value of life.

*　*　*

One night, my mom gave me five pesos to buy a half cup of soy sauce from the nearby, tiny sari-sari store. I was holding the cup in one hand and the money in my other hand.

As I was walking down the hilly side, I dropped and lost the money in the dark street. I looked for it for about 20 minutes before I had to face my mom and two brothers who had been waiting for the soy sauce to make the dish for our dinner.

After looking in vain for the money, I walked into the house without the soy sauce. With fear in my voice, I told my mom what happened. My mom gave me a flashlight and told me to go back out in the dark to look for the money.

One thing was certain even before I went out there to look for the money again. There was no way I would find that money again, especially in that dark, hilly, and windy place! If I didn't produce the money, my mom would surely hit me again. I spent at least an hour outside looking for the money and praying to God to drop some money from heaven, so I didn't have to pay the consequences for losing that money.

Tired and fearful, I went back home empty handed. I already knew what was waiting for me.

My mom stepped outside and cut up some guava tree branches and started hitting me with those until my skin bled. I wondered to myself if other children went through abuse like this!

* * *

The next day, I went to school by riding on a jeepney, a jeep used as transportation to all the people in the barrio. With a lunch that I packed myself, I was ready for school. I remember the other kids would make fun of me and my food (fish and rice wrapped with banana leaves), different than their freaking sandwiches in nice lunch boxes.

At school, I continued to struggle with school work. At my age, I was very behind in learning the basics. Other kids my age already knew how to read and write well, while I was still having a hard time learning the alphabet.

Mrs. Campos, my third grade teacher, saw my potential. She knew I just needed guidance. So, she personally offered to take me under her wing. She tutored me outside of school at her house. After weeks of voluntarily tutoring, just coming from her kind heart, I was finally catching up on reading and writing. She was one of those people who was willing to help me on her own time.

Soon after, Mrs. Campos asked me if I wanted to live with her and her husband at their house. I was brimming tears with happiness. I hurried home to tell my mom. She didn't even flinch when I told her. I guess she figured that she couldn't help me with school like Mrs. Campos.

After living with Mrs. Campos, I was doing much better in school. Mrs. Campos and her family were very nice to me. I felt the love I was missing in my own family. She also taught me how to pray for the first time in my life. The arrangement of living with her and her family didn't last long because my mom came and picked me up from the Campos family after one month. I guess my mom was jealous because I was doing well in school. So, off I went back to Gordon Heights with my mom.

* * *

We had to move again to another place since the little house we were renting was being sold by the owner. We moved to a little house on Block 1. We were across from a family that was very close to us, and their daughter, Jane and I became close friends. I used to babysit her and her two siblings all that time. Joy and I were like sisters; we became best of friends and stayed friends for many years.

This time, Jared left us and moved up to the mountain to make charcoal for a living. That left my mom, David, and me in that tiny house in Block 1. My school trips on a jeepney continued. I had to walk from our house up a steep hill for 25 minutes to meet the jeepney ride for the 30 minute ride to my school.

* * *

I still don't know why my mom would hit me for the slightest reasons. One time, she really got mad at me and started hitting me with a piece of wood. That piece of wood landed on my kneecap, resulting in a really bad knee injury, so bad that I had to use a cane to walk.

As usual, I was made to promise not to tell anyone...not to open my mouth! This is another secret that I had to keep from everyone. At school, my teacher saw me limping, having a hard time walking, and using a cane for support. She asked me what happened. I said, "Nothing." Then she placed her hand on my face, lifted my chin, looked at me in the eye, and asked me again what happened. I just said I fell down and landed on my knees.

Without telling me, I knew my teacher had a feeling I had been abused back then. In the Philippines, we didn't have CPS (Child Protective Services) to protect us; I had to deal with it on my own.

My teacher said she needed to see my mom to talk about how well I was doing in school. When I told my mom that, she looked at me and said, "Did you tell your teacher what happened?"

I said, "No, Mama, I didn't."

After the teacher-parent meeting, we left the school for the day, and I was taken by my mom to this old lady. A witch doctor who supposedly could heal anything.

This old lady took a needle, placed it on the fire, and poked it in my swollen knee. My knee was so infected that green pus came out of it. The witch doctor knew just what to do. I'm not sure what she put on my infected knee, but I was able to walk without pain the next day. This was a big relief for me, especially since my other knee was also bad from a previous injury when I was chased by a big mongrel dog, while climbing a fruit tree in the neighborhood.

*   *   *

David moved out of the house on Block 1. My mom was so mad at him for leaving her that she lit a candle on our doorstep to signify someone had just died. Now it was only my mom and me.

I finished third grade and was looking forward to fourth grade. My mom went back to work at the nightclub again. Since there was no one to look after me when she went to work at night, she took me up the mountain, where Jared had his own tiny little house, and left me with him during summer vacation.

At this point, I thought Jared was better than David…only to be proven wrong. On one rainy night, as I slept next to my brother on the floor, I felt his hand groping my body. I pushed him away. He grabbed me. I could scream, but no one would hear me. We didn't have neighbors, so it didn't matter even if I screamed at the top of my lungs; no one would hear my cry for help.

It happened again! A 20 year old raped a 9 year old. I felt betrayed by my entire family. How could all three of them abuse me? I am my mom's daughter and my brothers' sister! Why? They took my dignity! My virginity!

I was just so drained, I couldn't even shed a tear. I wanted to cry, but no tears were coming down my face. I hated them so much for what they did to me. I asked God. "Where are you?

Is this really my life's path, to live in fear, frustration, and sorrow?" I was just so tired of what was happening in my life. I turned to God to just take me, to let me be there with HIM in heaven. I was very helpless with no one to turn to.

The shame I felt made me feel so dirty. I thought scrubbing my skin would get rid of the dirt! Only to realize that no matter how hard and how much I scrubbed my skin, nothing was going to change in my life. All I knew was that my life was never going to change.

The three weeks I stayed with Jared were three weeks of hell. I was sexually, physically, and mentally abused during this horrible time. I did all the household chores. Although he didn't rape me again, he would hit me with any object he could find. One of my chores was cooking rice. We cooked rice using three big rocks and wood. One time, I burnt the rice. Cooking like this is not an easy task; you can't tell when the rice is done except by watching it constantly. Once you missed that exact time, you'll burn the rice. When I made this mistake, he used it as an excuse to beat me.

*   *   *

At the end of three weeks, my mom came and picked me up. In anger, she cut my hair in an ugly, coconut shape. I had long hair that reached past my waist line. I was so proud of my long hair. I guess cutting my hair so short in a coconut shape was some sort of punishment from my mom. At school, even with my beautiful, long hair, kids were making fun of me. It got worse when I showed up with my hair in such an ugly shape. Sometime, I would wear a turban to cover my hair.

When she got me home, she told me to go inside a rice sack (a coarse rough kind of cloth). She tied the knot with a long sturdy rope and threw the rope over the beam of the house, with me inside. I felt like an animal ready to be slaughtered by the hunter.

There were no excuse for what they did to me as a child. They scarred me for life. I was supposed to say nothing because this is my family. My family was supposed to protect me, instead they hurt me themselves.

At this point in my young life, I believed that it was never going to get better because bad things were always happening to me.

CHAPTER 4

Enough is Enough!

"Nothing is permanent in this wicked world,
not even our troubles."

- Charlie Chaplin

When I was ten years old, we moved again. This time way up into the mountains. My family found some land and built a little house for all four of us. Fred, my mom's boyfriend who she met at a nightclub, moved in with us a few months after they started dating, making a total of five occupants. I wasn't happy at all to see him there because my past taught me not to trust him, but there was nothing I could do.

Fred confirmed my fears when he tried to rape me. He didn't succeed because I screamed until my mom woke up. The next morning, I tried to tell my mom what her boyfriend was trying to do to me while I was sleeping. She said I was lying to her. She didn't even give me a chance to explain to her. I knew then that all that had happened to me by my two brothers would have to stay a secret forever. No one would ever know my past.

*   *   *

We lived so much farther from my school. I was determined to continue school, even though there were times when I didn't have the desire and there was lack of interest. It was better than staying home and doing nothing. The alternative was that I could end up like my mom, who couldn't read or write. So, I forced myself to go to school to get an education.

In fifth grade, even though I was struggling with school and my homework, I pushed myself to do better in school. However, I continued to be bullied. Kids at school saw that my school clothes were not as pretty as theirs. I didn't have a nice lunch bag; instead, my lunch was wrapped in banana leaves. I was called names. They called me ugly and pointed out the scars on my arms and legs. The bullying comments stayed with me for a very long time. For a long time, I refused to put on shorts because people might look at the scars on my legs.

One day, the bullying just got to be too much. I had more than enough! There were two girls in particular who picked on me, called me names, and made fun of me because of my food and the way I looked. As soon as they put their hands on me, I pushed them. I fought back.

I'd been used and abused by my own family. Somehow, I felt too weak to fight back, maybe because they are my family, my own flesh and blood. However when it came to others, like these two kids bullying me, I seemed to know how to fight back!

When I fought back against those two bullies, I got in trouble at school. I was suspended for one week. I had to go home and explain to my mom my ripped clothes and how it happened. Of course, she didn't believe me, so yes, she hit me again!

One thing I did not tell her was that I got suspended from school. I pretended I was going to school everyday of that whole week of suspension. To pass the time away, I would go to the park, sleep, and just hang around until it was time to go home. My mom would ask me if I had any homework, and I would always say no. That week went by quickly.

When I returned to school, my teacher wanted to see my mom. My mom came to the school and found out everything. Needless to say, she was furious. During the whole time my mom and I were walking from school to our house, she was pinching me and kept telling me that I lied to her and that I was going to suffer the consequences. I tried to explain to her that I was bullied and that I was just defending myself. It didn't make a difference since she didn't listen to any of that.

Once we got home, my mom closed all the windows and started hitting and beating me up all over my body with guava branches. All I could hear was her repeatedly saying, "This teaches you a lesson to not ever lie again!"

Fighting back against my mom was not even on my mind. I loved my mom so much that fighting back would be disrespectful. I just took the beating.

*　*　*

During summer break between fifth and sixth grade, I helped my mom with her work, doing laundry for other people. That was one way for us to earn a living. We also did gardening. We planted vegetables and sold them later. Mom would tie them up in bulks and bundles, and I would go to the barrio to sell them.

That was my daily routine during summer break. I had to work to make money for the family.

I didn't have the life of a normal child my age where I could be just be a child. I didn't have time to play kickball, dolls, or just plain be with other kids. I didn't see any other kid doing what I was doing...working at such a young age! I became jealous of other kids, and I stayed jealous for a long time.

I dreamed that someday I would get out of there, maybe even find myself in America - someday! I prayed to God every night to watch over me and give me the life that I so deserved. I never lost faith despite all the awful things that happened to me.

* * *

As for school, although I was enrolled in sixth grade, I lost interest. I knew that even though I had a strong desire to go to higher education, my chances were slim to none. No matter what I did, it wouldn't make a difference. Nothing I would do would make my mom love me anyway.

I started skipping school. My "school" days were spent sleeping in the park and hanging out doing nothing. I would go home at the same time school was dismissed. My mom had no idea what I was doing.

One day, I saw the mayor of our town handing out food to the townspeople. You had to have a ticket from the Red Cross so you can receive the food. To get the ticket from the Red Cross, there was another line you had to go into.

There I was with my ticket, standing in line in the pouring rain…waiting for the handout brown bag of goodies…food!

With the heavy bag of food, I took the 25 minute jeepney ride up to the nearest jeepney stop to our house. Then I had to walk uphill with the heavy stuff on my back for another 25 minutes. I came home with the brown bag full of food and happily gave it to my mom. She asked where I got the food, so I told her. I said, "Aren't you happy for me, Mama?" I knew she was happy because we desperately needed food. Sadly, she didn't show any joy or pride. Her answer was, "Go fetch some water from the well to fill our big barrel." And that was it!

That night, Fred, Mom's boyfriend, came home drunk. At dinner, he kept looking at me every time I put food in my mouth. I just bowed my head and continued eating, so I didn't have to look at him. After dinner, I would watch my mom give Fred a bath using the water I took the time to fetch from the well outside. It was sickening to watch this scenario. If my mom only knew that this man had tried to rape me! I didn't want this man in our house or in our lives. Just like with my traumatic experiences with my two brothers, I was helpless. I never said anything about it…keeping it a secret for a very, very long time.

The things that I heard at night between my mom and this man was more sickening. They fought all of the time and yelled horrible things at one another. They didn't care that a child was listening to their awful fights. I couldn't even look at my mom in the mornings. I was the one who was embarrassed!

I wanted to leave, but where would I go? I had no one to turn to!

*   *   *

After two weeks, my mom found out about me skipping school all the time. I have no idea how she found out, but she did. Needless to say, the beatings continued. My skin bled from the hitting. I was trying to protect my previously beat up, injured knee from being hit as Fred just stood there laughing at me while my mom was beating me up.

That same day, my mom commanded for me to fetch water from the artesian well so our huge water barrel would be filled. So, I started pumping water and filling two five gallon cans to fill the big oil barrel that held at least 50 gallons of water. So, I was carrying 10 gallons of water on each trip. I made five trips to fill that barrel with the cans hanging from a bamboo stick carried over my shoulders. This was ongoing as long we needed water for our everyday use.

On that particular water fetching, our neighbor approached me. She told me that she knew what my mother had been doing to me. She could hear me crying often. She was helpless to come to my aid. She said, "If I were you, with all the things they're doing to you, I would run away from your mean mother."

I told her, "I love my mother so much, I cannot leave her."

As I was pumping to fill the last bucket of water on my last trip to the house, something must have clicked in me because that night I decided enough was enough. This was the time!

It was getting dark. They were in the house when I managed to sneak out, running in the dark as fast as I could away from my mom and Fred. I was running towards my freedom!

I did not even notice that I had no shoes; all I had were the clothes on my back. I listened to that lady and ran as fast as I could. I was running into the opposite direction where my mom and Fred would not even think I would go.

Where would I go at this time of night? I remembered somewhat of a "safe" place under the bridge at the park. By now, I knew the parts of the park already. The water under the bridge was very smelly and stinky, but it didn't matter. It provided a safe haven for me...my refuge!

I fell asleep there, and I can't even remember how long I was sleeping in that place. I woke up hungry and thirsty. So, I went to the public open market and begged for food. The vendors shooed me away. I managed to take an apple or two when they were not looking. I guess someone saw me, so I started running away with the police chasing me. I've never run so fast in my life! Thankfully, the police didn't catch up with me!

I became HOMELESS!

Without food to eat, I would scavenge the trash to find something...just something to eat. I do believe that God was with me the whole time. I felt so safe somehow in my hiding place...the place I used to hang out when I was skipping school. One thing that was a blessing to me was the availability of a bathroom and running water in that park, so I was able to wash up. The running water was more than good enough for me to drink.

For the first time in my life, I was not scared. Even sleeping alone in the dark under the bridge somehow felt safer than being with my own family. I always knew God was with me and my guardian angels were watching over me. I was free at last from my mother, Fred, Jared, and David! I promised myself that I will never go back to my family again!

CHAPTER 5

Finding Kindness

*"I am not what happened to me,
I am what I choose to become."*

- C.G. Jung

As I continued my quest for food while living on the streets, I started walking towards the cinema. I hoped that I could find food that people threw in the garbage cans. I had no luck, and I was getting hungrier and hungrier. I saw a lady carrying a box of sandwiches; she was obviously delivering them for sale to the cinema. I approached her to see if she had an extra sandwich for me. Unfortunately, there were none.

Although I wasn't able to get a sandwich that first night, I learned that persistence pays off. I also realized that I needed more than a sandwich, I needed to find a way to survive on my own. I watched her for days delivering sandwiches to the cinema. On the third day, I had the courage to ask her if she was looking for help making the sandwiches. She said she wasn't.

The next day, I saw her taking back the old sandwiches. I asked her if I could have some. She gave me some since she was going to throw them away anyway.

The fourth time that I asked her if she needed help, she finally said yes. She asked me where I lived and where I slept. She had no idea I was sleeping on a cardboard box just behind the cinema billboard, wearing the same clothes that I was wearing when I left home about ten days ago. She also had no idea that I hadn't eaten food except the few times I could sneak anything to eat from the market place.

"Are you serious? Aren't you afraid at night?" she asked in disbelief!

The sandwich lady took pity on me and offered to let me stay with her and help her with her sandwich business. She said all she could offer me was a place to stay; she couldn't afford to pay me for helping with her business. All I said was that she didn't have to pay me, that I would work for free as long as I had a place to stay and food to eat. I promised to even clean her house, cook, and do laundry for her as long as she let me stay with her. I assured her that she wouldn't regret it.

This kind lady lived on the opposite side of Gordon Heights. She started asking me more questions about how I got to where she found me. She wanted to know why I ran away. At that point, I didn't want to tell her my life story and told her so.

*   *   *

We put the sandwiches in a cooler to stay fresh. Then I carried the cooler of sandwiches to sell at the main military base's gate. I started meeting many people. There were a lot of working women waiting by the gate for their boyfriends who were coming off of their ships.

My entrepreneurial passion was probably born here as the sandwich lady allowed me to sell the sandwiches to a point where I could make profit. During my childhood, I was always struggling, but this was something that I was good at! I felt proud of myself and believed this could be my way out of a bad life.

One day, the sandwich lady told me that my mom was looking for me. My heart started pounding. I wasn't going to break the promise to myself not to ever go back to my family again. A promise I made to myself when I was sleeping under the bridge. I told the lady that I would just get something from the store and that I'd be back right away. Instead, I went back to my hiding place under the bridge where I felt safe and away from my mother and Fred.

* * *

Eventually, I decided to try to make money at the base again. I'd saved up some of the money from selling sandwiches and used it to buy sodas. I sold the sodas at the base's gate and made some tips. It was going really well, but after a few weeks, while I was standing by the main gate, I spotted Fred. I was desperate to find a place to hide. There was a lady talking long distance at a nearby payphone. In a panic, I hid behind this lady and asked her not to move. Fred started walking towards the phone and spotted me. He grabbed me by hair and said, "We've been looking for you for a while now!"

We rode the jeepney all the way home. My mother was furious. I knew that my life was over. She started cutting guava leaves and began hitting me. At that point, I didn't flinch; I just took the beating. The next morning, my mother had a load to wash for Mr. Wong. Fred, Mama, and I walked to the stream to wash the clothes. For some reason, my mother forgot some of the laundry at the basin, so she told me to go back to get the clothes. "Don't do anything stupid like running away again!"

I looked her in the eyes, "I won't, Mama, I promise." Something clicked again; instead of picking up the clothes, I ran in the opposite direction. I just couldn't go back to living with my mom and Fred, so I went back to the bridge to hide.

*   *   *

During this time, I still had a little money saved from selling sandwiches and sodas, so I was able to buy food to eat. The same night around midnight, I started walking towards the main street, Magsaysay Avenue. That is when I saw Charina with her boyfriend. I used to sell sandwiches to Charina at the military base's entrance gate. I also ran small errands for her and her friend at that time. She immediately recognized me, "What are you doing in the middle of the night? Don't you have a place to stay?" I told her I didn't have a place go. As it was really getting late, she invited me to go with her to her apartment.

Charina found me wandering around downtown Olongapo City and rescued me! That night with my head bowed down, all I could tell her was that I ran away from home, as I didn't think it was the right time to tell her and her roommate, Cora, more of my story.

The next morning, I woke up very early before everyone else and started doing their household chores, like cleaning the apartment and doing the dishes. I was just so grateful that Charina and her friend took me in. I asked her if I could stay with her and Cora.

They asked questions again, as it was not normal for a young girl to be wandering alone at night. The street was not a place for a very young girl my age to just be pacing around with nowhere to go. I told them about my "home" under the bridge. I lost track of how long I stayed with Charina; I stopped counting after seven days.

I was longing for a place to stay where I'd be safe, so when the ladies asked me what I was going to do with my life, I told them I would like to stay with them. After they talked, they said yes, but that they couldn't pay me. I told them that I didn't need to get paid. In return, I would clean house, do the dishes, cook for them, and do other housework that they would like me to do…as long as I had a place to stay. I didn't mind at all that the only place I could sleep on was their couch! This was way more comfortable than sleeping on the ground under the bridge in the open space.

Days became weeks, weeks became months! Months became a year!

* * *

One day, I was washing clothes by hand in the back of the house. I heard a knock on the door, then a familiar voice…that of my mother! Charina opened the door. My heart was pounding! I didn't want to go back to my mom. When I heard the door knock, I knew I had to do something. I knew I could not be seen by her, so I climbed up into the back of a concrete wall and up by the roof of the apartment. I heard my mother say to Charina, "I will come tomorrow to see if Nelda is here." I knew she would come back, so I hid up on the galvanized roof for two solid days, enduring the rain, heat, and the cold, until I knew that my mother wouldn't come back for me.

I was no longer going to be a victim of my mother's abuse! I knew I would do whatever it took to make a better life for myself. Although I had hope and determination, I would still face many struggles in my young life.

CHAPTER 6

Abused Again

"Hope has two beautiful daughters. Their names are anger and courage; anger at the way things are, and courage to see that they do not remain the way they are."

— St. Augustine

For a year, I was able to enjoy a life of safety and support as I lived with Charina. Then she had to leave for the USA with her new husband. Charina took me to her parents' house in Manila. I was to take care of her young 5 year-old son who was left with her parents. I was fine with that, only to find out that I was going to do more than babysitting. Cleaning house, washing clothes (by hand), and cooking for everyone in the household was expected from me.

One of the occupants of that household was Charina's brother, who was about 4 years older than me. I was 12 at that time, so he was 16. Everything was fine, but when I turned 13, something changed...my body changed. I was becoming a teenager! I started getting uncomfortable with the way Charina's brother looked at me.

As time went by, I had to do more and more work around the house. I was a maid to all four people in that household. They had control over what I should be doing. How I missed Charina! I didn't complain at all because I didn't know any better. I had to make the best of the situation as they promised to send me to school to finish sixth grade.

School didn't happen. Instead, I was a slave for four years!

I suffered more than I could take as a child. I was hoping for a better life as I grew older, but things were not better yet. I continued to work for this family. I took the awful "servant" treatment. I wasn't allowed to eat with the family, instead I had to eat the leftovers in the kitchen.

Here I was with no education; I couldn't read and write well, or tell time. I was basically illiterate at that point. I fully understood why they didn't send me to school; if they did, there would be no one to do all the "maid's" chores!

As for Charina's brother, thank God, he never succeeded in raping me, but every chance he got to touch me, he surely did. I found out that he poked a hole in the bathroom to watch me shower. How sick is that? That was my life with this family!

While living with Charina's family, the thought of running away crossed my mind several times.

At one point, I even went to the nearest place that I could find in the neighborhood. It was a convent. I don't think becoming a nun was a destiny for me, as the steel door didn't open when I knocked on their door. I gave up after a few tries. It wasn't meant to be.

Although the church was not my destiny, I still kept my faith in God and knew he would provide a way out of the traumatic life I endured as a child. I knew I couldn't give up on my dreams of living a happy life away from those who would hurt me.

CHAPTER 7

A Surprising Way Out

*"We cannot start over, but we can begin now,
and make a new ending."*

- Zig Ziglar

After four years, when I was 16 years old, Charina came back to the Philippines to take her son to the States to live with her and her new husband. I was glad to see her. In my wildest dreams, I thought that she would take me with her to the U.S. as well, but since I'm not related to her, that didn't happen.

Charina took me to Olongapo City to visit her friend, Cora. Cora was still in the old place where I stayed before with her and Charina. Charina said she would find me a man to marry, so I could join her in the States. I had nothing to lose, so I agreed.

In Olongapo City, we stayed at the Crystal Place for two weeks. During this time, Charina invited me to go with her and Cora to the Mariners' Club inside the military base. We were dressed very nicely. Charina made sure I ironed her dress really well.

At the club, Charina was going around to see her friends, leaving me sitting alone at the table. I noticed a man with thick bifocal glasses looking in my direction. The music started to play, and this man got up and came over to our table. He asked me to dance. I said, "No, thank you."

I didn't want him to think I was a prostitute, which I am not and never was. The music started playing again, and again he got up and came to my table. Charina was not back yet. This man asked me again, "May I have this dance?" Finally, I said yes. It was a slow dance.

By this time, Charina was back and saw me dancing with this man. He introduced himself as Roger and asked my name. For the first time in my life, I heard someone tell me how beautiful I was. I never really saw myself in the mirror and notice how I looked.

When the music stopped, this man invited me to his table, but I refused nicely. He was okay with that. When I sat down at our table, Charina told me to ask Roger for a date. I said no, even if it was a great chance to ask for one because Charina figured Roger would be a way for me to get myself out of Olongapo and out of the Philippines.

Roger came to our table and asked me again to dance with him. I was getting more comfortable with him. He seemed like a nice person. Then he asked me if I would like to join him the next day for a beach picnic with just the two of us. I asked Charina if it was okay, and she told me to say yes, so I did.

After just less than 24 hours of knowing me, on May 16, 1976, after our picnic lunch, Roger got down on his knees and proposed, asking me to marry him. I didn't know what he was doing.

The mention of marriage took me by surprise, as we barely knew each other. It didn't matter to Roger. He said he knew me well enough already to ask me to be his wife. I found it strange.

I asked Roger, "How could you marry me when you don't even know who I am, my background and everything about me?" He was very insistent. Before I could decide and agree to his marriage proposal, I told him, "Let me tell you everything about me, and then tell me if you still want to marry me after hearing my story."

So there I was, telling my whole life story to Roger, from the rapes, running away from home, the abuses from my own family, enslaving by Charina's family, and the many painful experiences in between.

"Now, do you still want to marry me?" I asked Roger. His answer was a resounding, "Yes!"

To him, my past did not matter. What mattered most was the now, the present, this moment! He believed that for me to be able to get away from all of those past memories and make something positive out of the painful past was the most important thing.

When I heard that from Roger, I knew God had given me the opportunity of a lifetime. I said yes to the marriage proposal! I was engaged to be married to Roger. He's the reason I got out of that place, Olongapo City, a reminder of my painful past!

When I came home from the picnic, I told the news to Charina - I was getting married. She was shocked! She couldn't believe that my life was about to change forever in such a very short time.

Charina said she was happy for me, but she believed that when I got to the USA eventually that I would live with her. I told her, "I am marrying this man to be with him and not to live with you!"

She got mad that I talked back at her. Now she started talking about me owing her, that she was the one who found my man for me. Not true! Roger was the one who found me!

* * *

Since I was underage at 16, Roger's Commanding Officer wasn't able to marry us. I had to get a letter of consent from my mother. Roger understood the situation.

The next day, I went to see my mother to get the marriage consent signed, basically stating that it was alright for her to give me up to marry Roger. This was one of the few times my mother was happy around me. She gladly signed the consent papers.

I met with Roger the next day. Our wedding day was set. I also told Roger about Charina and what she had said. Roger got mad, so I told him that it was not worth it to argue with her.

Next up was my trip back to Manila, to Charina's family to gather all my things that I left behind. The family was shocked and upset about what had happened so suddenly. I really didn't care because I had done more than enough slaving for them all those years. Now, it was time for me to have a better life. In my haste to just get out of there, I just didn't want to spend any more minute with them, so I left all my stuff there. I didn't care.

I left and never looked back.

CHAPTER 8

Love & Betrayal

*"You may be deceived if you trust too much, but you will
live in torment if you don't trust enough."*

- Frank Crane

Roger and I were married on May 22, 1976 in the church in
Olongapo City. The ceremony was very simple, nothing fancy.
I just wore my regular clothes and only had Charina and Cora in
attendance. We had our honeymoon at the Admiral Suite in Sta.
Rita, which is about a 10 minute drive from Olongapo City. Our
wedding night was quite an experience. I didn't know what to
expect as to what goes on during such a night. I didn't know I had
to sleep with my husband.

I locked myself inside the bathroom. Roger knocked on the
bathroom door and asked me to open the door. "You're my wife
now," he lovingly said to me.

The next morning, I had a lot of explaining to do. I got scared.
I apologized to Roger and assured him that it wasn't him, but me.
I asked for more patience from him. Being the great man that
he was, he was very nice about the whole thing. "I'm sorry that I
rushed you into this; it won't happen again. When you're ready, just
let me know." I guess I wasn't ready for all of the changes that were
happening in my life in just a matter of weeks.

Roger and I found a place to live - a cute little apartment right next door to Cora's apartment.

With my dependent ID, I was now able to get in and out of the military base. Roger was being assigned to be at sea for 45 days in the Japanese waters with July 16 as his "coming back" day.

For the two weeks before he left, Roger and I had a great time getting to know each other better, even though the marriage wasn't consummated at this point. Roger was very patient about that, and I loved him for it.

* * *

Roger soon left for his assignment on June 7th. I was busy with all the things I needed to do before our move to the United States. That meant a lot of going back and forth to the military base to fulfill many of the requirements in preparation for my trip to the USA as a wife and military dependent. This included immunization shots and more paperwork.

One day in June, June 13 to be exact, I was very curious and excited at the same time. I went inside the base, explored, and looked around. Since my husband's rank was an E3, the amount of time I was allowed inside the base was limited.

As I was walking out of the base at about 6 pm, a Marine soldier started giving me a hard time about my ID card. He summoned me to go inside the office and said, "Are you even of legal age to be married?"

All I said to him was, "Mind your own business. What did I do wrong?"

He answered with, "I just wanted to see you." Without saying a word, I turned around and left. Little did I know that this soldier would play an important role in my life.

The next day, I had a dental appointment inside the base as part of my requirements, in addition to all the shots I had to get. Who did I see at the gate but this Corporal Marine from the day before, checking everyone's ID. From his name badge, I learned that his name was Teddy.

The line I was in was long, so I switched to the shorter one. What do you know, this fellow also switched lanes to the one I was in! Now what would be his excuse when he gives me a hard time with my ID? Then came my turn to be checked for my ID. He looked at me and said, "Do you know that you're beautiful?"

I ignored what he said, and I just plainly replied back to him with, "What do you want?"

He said, "Nothing, I just want to talk to you." I really didn't have time for all these pleasantries. I just wanted my card back. He gave it back, and I just turned around and left. I knew he was still looking at me as I walked away. I kept on walking and was determined not to pay attention.

I didn't go to the base for a week until my next appointment was due for the TB shot. That meant that I had to go through the main gate again. I was praying to God that I wouldn't see Teddy again. But lo and behold, who would be there but Teddy! This time, he was bold enough to give his US telephone number, just in case I needed it when I got to the US. He said to look him up whenever I get there. Just to shut him up and leave me alone for good, I took his number.

On July 16, my husband came home from his long 45 day stint in Japan. He had a surprise for me - my wedding ring! It would be a deterrent for Teddy if he saw that wedding ring on my finger!

I was afraid to go to the base while Roger was home. I didn't want to go to the base and see Teddy there. Well, for the whole month that Roger was home, there was no sight of Teddy at the main gate! I guess he was stationed somewhere else. I was so relieved.

After only two months together, on about September 16 (just a few days before my birthday), Roger had to go back to the US for good. His tour in Olongapo City, Philippines was over. His new assignment was in Miramar Air Base in San Diego, California, which was also now my destination.

During the time that Roger was with me, I saw Teddy from time to time. I was usually with my husband. I knew what that look on Teddy's face was telling me whenever he saw me with my husband. It was the "You should be with me" kind of look. I mentioned to Roger about Teddy giving me a hard time. Roger said, "He's just jealous because you're mine and not his."

Roger had to leave me in the Philippines while my papers were being worked on. I was scared of being alone during the months until my scheduled departure on December 2, 1976.

With me by myself, I had to do things like check my mail inside the base. Every time I'd go to the base, there was always Teddy, who seemed to know that my husband had left for the US for good.

Now Teddy had the courage to approach me and ask if we could meet. I always had to say no. I must have told him no at least ten times, but there was no sign of him giving up on asking me. On the 11th time, he invited me to a football game that he was going to watch since he was on duty call that night. He asked if I could at least watch the game with him.

I said, "I can't come inside the gate after hours," thinking that could discourage him. Unfortunately, he was resourceful. He already thought of how to let me in after hours. He would have his buddy let me in. He would just call the main gate. I thought about this for a few hours before the game was to start at 6 pm.

After much thought, I decided that I would go see him. I guess I was attracted to Teddy since he was a gentleman, very persuasive, and just wouldn't give up. So, his buddy let me in. There I was sitting on the bleacher watching the game with Teddy. When the game was over, he walked me to the gate to make sure that no one gave me a hard time about my ID card.

The next day, I saw him again at the base. This time, I could feel my heart pounding and felt those butterflies in my tummy. I didn't know what that meant. I only experienced those feelings when I saw him.

The following week, he asked me to meet him at the pool after my errands. He said I could bring my bathing suit if I wanted to. I decided to go to the pool, even though I didn't know how to swim. I just stayed by the ledge. I didn't think I was doing anything wrong since I was only having a conversation with him in a public place by the pool.

When it was time to go, he went to his duty call that started at 6pm. Before I went home, I asked for his T-shirt as a souvenir. In the Philippines, we like to ask for souvenirs (small little remembrances) from friends we meet, whether we'll see them again or not. In my mind, my request was made with good intentions as I saw him as a friend, nothing more.

At that time, I was staying with Roger's boss' wife and her family. She just happened to be visiting at that time. So, I was staying with them until I was to fly to San Diego, CA. She and I were going to leave together.

I had Teddy's shirt with me, and Roger's boss' wife found out about it. She wrote my husband and told him I was cheating on him. It wasn't even true as we were just friends. Nothing happened between Teddy and I, not even a kiss. This woman ruined my life.

Roger fell for that gossip and true enough, he stopped sending me my monthly allotment. Roger left me with only $500 that I was expecting to use towards my airfare to go the states. Shortly after, Teddy left Olongapo City for good.

This was one of those early beginnings when I started losing trust to people. Although my family had never been there for me, others throughout my life had been there for me. Up until this lie and betrayal, I had trusted most people. I told myself that thinking that everybody is your friend is just not true. I guess she was jealous of me and Roger didn't really trust me. I know in my heart that I didn't do anything wrong.

CHAPTER 9

A Gift of a Lifetime

*"At whatever straws we must grasp, there is always a
time for gratitude and new beginnings."*

- J. Robert Moskin

Although I had no one waiting for me in the US, I knew I still had to find a way to use this opportunity to get to America and a better life. I went to Manila to get my passport and my visa from the U.S. Embassy. All that was missing was the money to buy myself a ticket to America.

After getting my passport, I realized I had nowhere else to go except back to Olongapo City until I found a way to get a ticket. I'd hoped that Roger would forgive me and send me enough to make it to the States.

The bus ride back to Olongapo City changed my life forever. I was sitting next to a very nice looking lady about 45 years of age. She noticed the big envelope I was holding. Then she asked me where I was going. I said, "I'm going to the US in a week." She said that I must be very excited, to which I replied, "Very much so as I have dreamed about this since I was 7 years old."

This lady must have sensed something was bothering me as she could probably see it on my face. She asked me if something was wrong. To answer her inquiry, I told her I was short of money to buy a ticket.

She asked me if I had to go right away to Olongapo City. I said, "I have to because I have to check my mail and see if my husband sent my allotment."

"What happens if you don't get your allotment?" she asked.

"I will be stuck in Olongapo City since my visa will expire."

She looked at me and invited me to go with her to her house not far from the terminal to have dinner with her and her children. She wanted to hear more of my story.

I thought to myself, "I have nothing to lose. So why not?" I asked her why she was inviting me, a stranger she barely knew, to her home.

This lady just looked at me and said, "I will change your life forever."

I had no idea what she meant by that. I asked her, "How?"

"I'd like to help you. Come to my house, stay for the night, and continue on to Olongapo City tomorrow."

By this time, I was silently freaking out! Here I am meeting this stranger on the bus and now she wants to help me? I asked again how she would help me. She said that the next day, she would take me to get my ticket for the U.S. at the Philippine Airlines office.

"But I told you I don't have enough money for the ticket. That's why I'm anxious to go back to Olongapo City to the base, so I can check my mail and see if my husband came to his senses. Maybe I will find my allotment check in the mail," I told her.

"I hear you. But why take that chance? If you go back to Olongapo City tonight and don't see the check in the mail, then you'll be stuck here in the Philippines. I am willing to co-sign for your ticket from the Philippine Airlines. You can pay me back when you get to the US," she explained.

I was dumbfounded as I sat in my seat on the bus. With tears in my eyes, I gave this lady the biggest hug I could give! There is a God after all, a God that has been watching over me my whole life!

* * *

I went with the lady to her beautiful home. We had dinner, and I stayed for the night. The next morning at around 10 am, we went to the Philippine Airline travel office. She told the lady there that she wanted to co-sign for "this young lady for her one-way ticket fly now pay later." The travel agent started typing and preparing all the paperwork, and then we were done!

My life was certainly changed forever! It was surreal, so unbelievable! Once again, I gave this lovely lady a big hug. With tears in my eyes, I told her that this was the nicest thing that I have been offered. With my life being a mess since I was 6 years old, this experience was a gift of a lifetime.

"You deserve it. Now go and get your things together as soon as possible; you have limited time."

"I will never forget you and what you did for me. I will pay you back every penny."

"I trust that you will keep your promise to make the payments to the agency. I just want you to have a great life in the States."

As we were saying our last goodbyes, I gave her another big hug. "Thank you," was all I could say. I was just in disbelief. As I was walking away, I turned around and she was gone...just disappeared so quickly!

I was so happy...holding my ticket...my ticket to change my life forever!

I went back to Olongapo City to gather my things, but most of all to check my mailbox to see if I had a letter or anything from my husband. It was empty.

I was very disappointed with Roger. I knew he was really mad at me. He didn't even listen to my explanation about how everything he heard was very untrue. He probably thought that since he wasn't sending me money for my ticket, that my visa would expire soon, that I would rot and be stuck in the Philippines. Little did he know that I met a miracle, that lady who helped me get my plane ticket.

I went to see my mother and said goodbye. The next day, December 2, 1976, was my departure to the United States. My mother, my brother David and his friend, Eddie, saw me off as I walked towards the gate at the airport.

I had no tears when I said goodbye. I promised myself I would never come back!

CHAPTER 10

The Kindness of Strangers

*"How beautiful a day can be when
kindness touches it."*

- George Elliston

After a very long flight, I arrived in Los Angeles!

It was around midnight, and I was alone with no one to pick me up from the airport. I just relied on a friend from the Philippines, Elise, who lived in the States. She was vacationing in the Philippines before I left, and she gave me a phone number of a friend to call if I needed a place to stay. If it wasn't for Elise, I wouldn't have anyone to contact when I arrived in the US. That phone number belonged to a certain Mrs. Patty Walker, who was a very good friend of Elise. I'd hoped to spend time with her in the States and thank her for her help. However, I found out that Elise was deported back to the Philippines, and I never had the chance to thank her.

I dialed the telephone number given to me by Elise. Mrs. Walker answered the phone. I told her my name and how I got her number. I also told her that I was at the airport, and I needed someone to pick me up if possible since I didn't have anywhere else to go. She must not have understood me or the broken English that I'd learned in school, so she gave the phone to her nurse.

I explained my situation to the nurse. Then the nurse said that there was no way Mrs. Walker could come and pick me up because she was paralyzed. I didn't even understand what "paralyzed" meant until the nurse explained it to me. The nurse must have further explained everything to Mrs. Walker because she came on the phone again and started talking to me. Mrs. Walker suggested that I stay at the airport for the night and then in the morning, I could take the bus to Van Nuys, which is on the other side of LA County.

I wasn't going to stay at the airport for the night. I still had a little bit of money left in my pocket, so I decided to look for a cheap hotel nearby. I figured I had enough to pay the hotel for one night. I hailed a cab to take me the nearest and cheapest hotel.

When the cab driver dropped me off, he said that hotel was not a good one. I was puzzled by what he meant by that. I could care less about the condition of the hotel; I just needed a place to sleep for a couple of hours. I asked him what was wrong with it. All he said was it was a very bad hotel and to make sure to lock my door. He said, "I will pick you up in the morning and take you to the bus stop for Van Nuys." I thanked him, and he left me there at the hotel.

The hotel was a little scary looking. I remembered what the taxi cab driver told me, so to take it further, I pushed the dresser towards the door to block it, so no one could come in.

The next morning, the cab driver was already waiting for me outside, ready to drive me to the bus stop. My first experience of a random act of kindness came from this cab driver who didn't even take my money. All he said was, "Welcome to America!" He was the very first person to welcome me!

As soon as I was dropped off at the bus stop, I was standing there looking around when a white Mercedes Benz pulled in front of me. The driver asked me if I needed a ride. Not getting a ride from a stranger was what was on my mind, so I said, "No, thank you."

This man just ignored what I said. He continued talking to me and asking me questions about where I was going and what bus was going in my destination. Before I could say anything, he reassured me to trust him. I told him I was going to Van Nuys. He said there was no single bus that goes that far. I would have to take four bus connections to get to Van Nuys, and it would take two hours. Then he said, "I'm heading that way anyway, I can go ahead and take you to your destination, right to Mrs. Walker's doorstep."

I took my chances again by trusting this nice gentleman. I said to him, "You're not going to do bad things to me, are you?"

He said, "No, young lady. I don't do that at all."

"But why me?" To which he answered that I looked very lost and like I was new in the States.

The conversation went on, and finally I asked what his name was. He just gave me his business card with his name and phone number. I didn't ask any more questions after that. I just sat there and guarded my papers (visa, etc.) and prayed to God to keep me safe. It didn't take him long to get to Mrs. Walker's house. He had a small talk with Mrs. Walker, who thanked him for giving me a ride and dropping me off safely.

At this point, the more I realized that everything in life is an opportunity. Everything happens for a reason. My belief in humanity, that there are really nice people on this planet, just made me more trusting. God has always been with me through this whole ordeal of my life.

* * *

I stayed with Mrs. Walker and slept on her couch. She was a quadriplegic who needed nursing care 24/7. I started watching how the nurse was doing the caregiving. I was thinking that maybe I could learn to help and care for Mrs. Walker, so she didn't have to pay the nurses.

After two weeks of staying with Mrs. Walker, I learned so much about caregiving and what the nurse was doing to help her. I told Mrs. Walker that I could help care for her. I asked her to please allow me to repay her for her kindness in taking me in when I didn't have any place to stay.

Mrs. Walker said that I didn't have to because she could afford to pay the nurse to take care of her. I begged her to at least let me try it for one week. If I couldn't and it was too much for me, then she could call her nurse again. I ended up doing a good job taking care of Mrs. Walker. I did everything I needed to do.

Meanwhile, Mrs. Walker was looking in the paper for job openings for me! One day, she found an ad for a live-in maid that paid $100/week. She told me to check the agency out. I said, "How about you? Who's going to take care of you?" She said not to worry about her because she could always call her nurse for assistance.

I started working as a live-in maid in Sherman Oaks and did so for four months. I knew that I wouldn't have any problem being a live-in maid. I was blessed to have found a job so quickly, in a matter of weeks, after moving to the United States. Having a job as a live-in maid was not difficult for me because it is what I did for many years in the Philippines. Although I should not have been treated as a maid when I was a child, it did give me the experience I needed to quickly find a good job.

For a young woman with no education, the money was really good. I was making $100 a week to clean, cook, complete the usual chores that I was familiar with, and take care of a 7 year old girl and a huge Great Dane.

* * *

Although I was very good at my job, I had to lie to get this job because one of the requirements was to be single. I didn't think it would be a problem since Roger was not a part of my life. However, I ended up having to tell them that I was married, but separated from my husband, when Roger found me at my workplace. He drove up from San Diego to apologize. He told me that he should have given me the benefit of the doubt and heard my side of the story. He tried to get me back, but I was still mad at him. I refused to go back with him since I was already settled in my new life. I told Roger that I couldn't go with him. He left with sorrow on his face. I knew he was hurt. If only Roger had listened to me and not those people who tried to ruin our lives together as a husband and wife.

Although Roger was disappointed, we both agreed that it would be best if we got a divorce. I'm happy to share that Roger and I became friends after the divorce. I will always appreciate the support and opportunities Roger brought into my life, but I knew after that first betrayal that we were not meant to be together forever and that there were other relationships waiting for me in the future.

CHAPTER 11

Rollercoaster of Love

"A person isn't who they are during the last conversation you had with them - they're who they've been throughout your whole relationship."

- Rainer Maria Rilke

After officially ending my relationship with Roger, I found Teddy's telephone number and address on a piece of paper in my suitcase. I called him, and we started talking on the phone almost everyday. After a month, he invited me to visit him in North Carolina. Needless to say, we got to know one another much better and our relationship blossomed.

After visiting for a week, he didn't want me to go back to California. He was already talking about getting our own place. It made him sad to think about possibly never seeing me again. I felt the same way, so I went back to California to give notice to my employer that I was quitting and moving to North Carolina.

In April, 1977, I packed my suitcase, said goodbye to Mrs. Walker, and thanked her for everything. After I said my goodbyes, I was headed for a new life in North Carolina with Teddy. We found a little place to live in a trailer. After five months, in September, Teddy was done in the Marines. He decided to move us to Boston, Massachusetts, where he was originally from.

Once we moved, I met his family. His mother, Marie B., wasn't really thrilled to meet me because I was Asian. I guess she wanted a Caucasian for a daughter-in-law. In spite of that, I got along well with everyone, including his six siblings.

I found a job in Boston, in a factory, in the printing department. It paid $1.89 per hour for a full time position. It was a low paying job, but I liked it because it allowed me to help pay our bills and send money back to family in the Philippines. Even though my mother had not been there for me during my childhood, I couldn't break with the cultural tradition of sending financial support back to family members that were left behind.

* * *

The first year together was beautiful, just perfect. I was so happy. However, a year after I moved in with him, Teddy started having some issues. He started drinking and doing drugs. Sometimes he wouldn't come home for days, so I was left alone in our little place.

I started becoming distant from Teddy. We had a lot of fights because of his drinking and use of drugs. I became angrier at him more and more everyday. This left me feeling so alone...eating and sleeping alone...existing in a lonely situation.

I asked myself so many questions: Is this how a couple should be? Did I make the wrong choice in life?

Just to feel something again, even if it was pain, I went into a deep depression. I started hitting myself. I started mutilating my body, stabbing myself with sharp pencils. I became bulimic and anorexic. This situation felt as if my experience in my own childhood abuse was happening all over again. I felt that life was repeating itself. I felt like I lost myself along the way and became weak. I couldn't control myself. The self stabbing, bulimia, and anorexia continued for four years until I was almost 20 years old.

Teddy stopped loving me! I became an emotional prisoner in my own world. Without Teddy, my life was in shambles.

With all these things going on in my life, I managed to continue working at the factory. We had to make a living.

I continued to live with Teddy and struggle with my feelings of hopelessness for four more years. Finally, I knew I had to make a change. I earned a one week vacation from my job, and knew I had to use this opportunity to get out of the abusive situation I'd found myself in. It was finally time to leave Teddy! I bought myself a one-way ticket back to California. I was thinking, "I should have stayed here instead of following my heart!" Sometimes, you have to learn the hard way to get the life you want!

* * *

When I arrived in California, I stayed with Mrs. Walker for a week because she was the only one I could run to. She was nice enough to take me in again after everything she had done for me when I first got to the states. Her health was declining, and she passed away soon after my visit. I was so glad that I got to see her one last time. I don't know what I would have done without her help.

Within a week, I found a job as a live-in maid again. I was so happy knowing my life was in order again. I loved Teddy so much, but I had to do what was best for me and leave him.

A month after I left Teddy, I called his father to say hello and see how Teddy was doing. He said Teddy wasn't doing well. He also said that Teddy missed me terribly and very sad that I left him.

I had to explain my side to Teddy's dad about what happened and why I left. All the drinking, drugs, leaving me for days, not being there for me when I needed him, making his friends more important than me AND what all these things did to me as a person! I became a prisoner in my own home, alone and depressed. Those bouts of hurting myself physically, the bulimia and anorexia! Four years of all these terrible things in our relationship took its toll. I had to leave to keep my sanity. I told him I endured that for four years. It was time to leave and start a new life in California. His father understood. I told him I'd be calling again sometime soon.

A week went by and, as I promised Teddy's dad, I called back. It so happened that Teddy was there. I guess his dad told him what I said to him. Teddy took the phone and was now talking to me. He begged me to come home. He pleaded and promised not to treat me like he did before. He told me that he'd be good to me. He threatened to jump off a bridge and kill himself if I didn't come home to him. This conversation and the crying on the phone took over an hour.

After a month of being away from him, one thing I knew was that I would always love him in spite of everything. I fell for his sobbing and pleading. I didn't want anything bad to happen to him. So, I flew back to Boston to be back in his arms.

* * *

When I came back from California, life was great. It got so much better when I became pregnant and gave birth to our first child. A wonderful little girl! A healthy 8.5 lb. and 21 in. bundle of joy! The best Mother's Day gift!

The birth of our little girl made me the happiest person in the happiest moment of my life. My little girl brought me back to life. This was what my life's journey was leading me to - having this precious little girl of mine. I looked at this baby and promised that I would always be there for her. I'd be the greatest mother she could ever have.

Teddy was so proud to be a daddy. Our little girl became the apple of his eye. Life in our household was wonderful. Everything went back to normal.

I doted on my daughter so much. I just wanted to be with my baby, so I didn't go back to work. I just wanted to be close to her. I wanted to be with her until it was time for her to go to college.

Two and a half years later, we had another child; a boy this time. This little boy would grow up to always protect me and his sisters. He was such a great little boy who wouldn't leave my side.

I love my children so much. When I look at my children, I always wonder how anyone could harm and abuse their children, their own flesh and blood. How could anyone, like my mother and brothers, hurt a child like they did to me?

As my children grew, time and time again, I always asked myself those questions. I just couldn't understand how any mother, or any family member, could abuse her own. I vowed that whatever I went through as a child in the hands of my own family would never ever happen to my children. My love for my children is even greater because of what happened to me.

CHAPTER 12

Returning to the Past

"It take a huge effort to free yourself from memory."

\- Paulo Coelho

In 1987, I finally became a citizen of the U.S.A. It was about time for me to visit the Philippines after 11 years of absence. I told Teddy that I wanted to visit my mother. I went by myself, leaving my two children with their dad.

I knew it was time for me to see my mother and try to deal with our problems. I wanted answers about what had happened in my childhood. I wanted to catch up with my mom and learn about all the things that happened while I was gone. I hoped I'd also have a good time and visit the beautiful places in the Philippines that I'd never been to before. I planned on taking my mother to her hometown of Mindanao; she used to tell me it was the most beautiful place in the world.

I also wanted to visit my third grade teacher, Mrs. Campos. I wanted to thank Mrs. Campos for what she had done for me. She had shown me the love and affection that I didn't receive from my family. I wanted to tell her that I was okay because she believed in me. She believed that someday, I could be someone. I wanted to thank her for her patience while teaching me how to pray, read, and write.

*   *   *

I arrived in the Philippines on April 2, 1987. My best friend, Jane, and my mother came to pick me up at the airport. As soon as I saw my mother standing there at the airport arrival gate, I started feeling sick to my stomach. I didn't know what was going on with me. Everything was coming back so quickly, and I couldn't handle all of the traumatic memories that flooded my mind when I saw her face.

It was a good thing that Jane was there. I was so glad to see her. It's hard to admit, but I could no longer speak my native language. Even if I try to speak Tagalog, what comes out of my mouth is in English. Jane was my translator.

I didn't feel anything when my mom hugged me. She was a stranger to me at that moment. Strange, but I didn't feel anything for my mom. I was supposed to be happy to be back in the Philippines, but I just wanted to hop on the next airplane and immediately go back to Boston to be with Teddy and our children.

As my mom, Jane, and I were sitting on the bus going to Olongapo City, I asked Jane, who was sitting next to me, if I could stay at her house for the three weeks that I'd be in the Philippines. She said of course. Jane had no idea about my childhood trauma, even though we were close friends who lived across the street from each other while growing up.

I was still experiencing jet lag. All I wanted to do was catch up on my sleep and relax after traveling. Well, none of this relaxing and sleep ever happened. That very same day, my mom argued with me in front of my friend's house. She was very upset that I was staying with Jane and her family.

She couldn't understand why I refused to stay with her. I just couldn't go back to that house where I had so many bad memories. I never told my mother that I nearly got raped by her boyfriend,

Fred. The traumatic memory was just too much for me. I had never told her, and it wasn't my intention to tell her until I was done visiting.

Right at that very moment, I started to shake when my mother put her hands on me. I was shaking uncontrollably. I was having a nervous breakdown! I started telling her some of things that happened to me as a child.

She couldn't understand what I was saying because I was speaking English. I had to say every word very slowly. In detail, I told her everything that happened to me during my childhood and about my struggles and hardships over the past 11 years in the States.

I explained to my mother, "Mama, the reason why I don't want to stay with you in that house is because of the bad memories I have; horrible things happened to me in that very house. Remember, you beat me up and hung me upside down! You cut my hair into an ugly coconut shape. You broke my knee when you hit me with a piece of wood and sent me away to an older woman to take care of me. One time, you left me downtown in Olongapo City and didn't come back for me. You locked me in the house with bars while you went to work. Did you know David and Jared raped me on separate occasions? That's why I ran away from you and Fred!"

After telling her everything what had happened to me as a child - raped by my two brothers and also abused by her as she beat me as punishment for every little thing, I felt release about myself knowing that for 11 years I was in so much pain and sorrow and shame about what my family has done to me as a child. After telling her all these things, she left without a tear in her eyes. So, I went to sleep, but hours later Mrs. Mendo woke me up and told me that my mother had gone crazy. Having said all of that to my mother, I felt so strong. I didn't feel afraid of speaking my feelings to her.

Jane and I went to see what was going on. My mother was very drunk and was "swimming" in the mud at 10:00 at night! Everyone in the neighborhood was there to witness this spectacle. I tried to pick my mom up and get her out of that mud, but she fought back. She was saying, "My daughter doesn't love me anymore." This reaction from her was the result of all that revelations I had with her three hours earlier. She felt so guilty about what she did to me and what happened to me in my childhood that she wanted to kill herself.

My mom was hysterical. I couldn't control her, so I slapped her across the face to put some sense into her. Then I poured cold water on her face to wake her up. The whole neighborhood was watching this ordeal; they were shocked. I'll never forget the look on their faces. In their minds, I was a rotten daughter for what I did to my mom.

This scenario continued for an hour until the arrival of my brother, Jared, who heard about the commotion from someone. Now I had another person to deal with. He asked me what I was doing to our mother. I just stood there and looked him straight in the eye and said, "Shut the hell up!"

"Why did you even come home?" he shouted back at me.

Without missing a beat, I looked at him again and asked one thing and one thing only. "Why did you rape me when I was 9 years old? I'd like to hear your answer coming from your own mouth!"

Another shock to the whole neighborhood watching this whole thing about me, my mom, and Jared. All Jared could say was, "It is all in the past."

I was furious. If I had a gun that night, I could have shot him for what he did to me. If David was there, I could have shot him too. I looked him in the eye and said, "I WAS YOUR LITTLE SISTER!" The whole place became silent. Then I left.

My path lead me to the church. It was midnight, and I was knocking on the church's door. I wanted to talk to a priest about what had just happened and what I did. The priest opened the door and let me in. I asked for forgiveness for what I did to my mother.

The priest said to me, "Nelda, you carried that cross on your shoulder all this time, including the last 11 years that you've been away. Now, it's time for your mother and brothers to carry that cross."

I left the church in tears. I went back to my friend's house crying. The next day, I packed my suitcase to go back home to Teddy and my children. Before this trip, Teddy and his family did not know about the traumatic experiences from my childhood. After this ordeal with my mom, I needed to tell Teddy everything and explain why I wanted to come back so quickly. Once he understood what I was dealing with, he was anxious for me to return home.

Instead of three weeks, I returned after four days. I was so happy to see Teddy and the kids.

I was home. Those four days released me from the nightmare of my life...finally!

CHAPTER 13

A Bright Future

"There are far better thing ahead than any we leave behind."

\- C.S. Lewis

Two weeks after my trip, Teddy told me we were moving to Venice, Florida! I hadn't even had the chance to unpack my suitcase from my trip to the Philippines, and here we were about to be on the road again.

After living in the Venice area for about a year, Teddy started doing heavy drugs. When he left me and the children for three months, it left us no choice but to move out of that house and move to a smaller one bedroom apartment.

Seven months after the kids and I left, Teddy wanted to come back to us. The way he did it was through our precious 7 year old daughter, our first born. He had her ask me to take her dad back. I told my daughter that I was only taking their dad back because of them, the children. If it was up to me, I would not have done so. For the sake of the kids, Teddy was back in our lives.

Our third child, a healthy and beautiful 8 lb. and 21 in. girl, was born in June, 1990. With all the things that our family was experiencing, Teddy just didn't have the patience like I have. I guess it was too much for him.

*   *   *

In September, he left for good, leaving me with three young children, including a 3-month old newborn. I said to myself, "Nelda, you can do this. It is nothing compared to what you have gone through in your life." I knew that God was testing me again to see how I could handle three children with three jobs. I had a job working for the school as a cafeteria lady for three hours, and then at 10:00, I would clean people's house for three hours before my children got out of school around 2:00 in the afternoon. By night, I would have someone babysit my three children while I worked as a waitress at a Japanese restaurant near our house. It was tough, but it didn't matter to me as long as I had my babies with me. I did whatever needed to be done. I knew that I had to be strong enough to take care my children because they are my life.

I made a promise to my children that I would always be there for them. They knew we were struggling financially, but knew I was working hard to provide for them. I remember my oldest daughter looking at the Barbie doll at a toy store. I said to her, "Do you want that, honey?"

My daughter said, "Mommy, it's okay, maybe someday." It broke my heart when she told me that she knew I had to work hard to get that doll for her. I did but not the Barbie, but was able to get her something similar.

I remember my son used to say to me, "Mommy, today is Wednesday. Kids eat for free!" So, I would dress them up and take them to a local restaurant where kids could eat all the food they wanted each Wednesday.

Along with financial challenges, raising and disciplining the children was also challenge for me. As a single mother, I disciplined my children the best way I could. I was strict, and my daughters couldn't understand why I was so strict. I have shared some of my story with my kids, but when they were younger, they couldn't really understand why I raised them the way I did. I was only protecting them from others that could harm them. For example, if my daughter wanted to go sleep over at her friend's house, I would need to speak to the parent first see if they were going to be home while she was staying at their home for the night. My daughter would be so mad at me because she thought I didn't have trust in her. It was not her that I didn't trust, it was the people outside our home whom I didn't trust.

Although being a single mother was incredibly difficult, I was a fighter. I never gave up. I made sure my children were taken care of, and I knew that someday, things would get better.

* * *

On July 13, 1991, I met Richard Crawford through my neighbor Carmen. I was having car problems and had no money to fix my car, so Carmen told me that she knew a guy who might be able to help. She told me to call him.

When I first met him, he had a huge smile on his face. He looked at my car and told me he could fix it. When I told him I didn't have much money, he said I could pay him a little at a time. A week after he fixed my car, he asked me out for a date. It was weird at first because he was my mechanic. I'd just been focused on getting my car fixed!

I was suppose to meet him around 9:00 at Cha Cha Coconut, a restaurant and nightclub, but I stood him up because I was afraid of bringing another man into my life. I didn't want my children to see a new man in their lives after what their father did to us by leaving. The next day, he came by to my house and said, "You didn't show up, what happened?" I told him I wasn't ready for another relationship. I had been single for just over a year, and I was not about to start another relationship. He told me to let him know when I was ready.

I wasn't sure I'd ever be ready. I had a one year old, my oldest was 9 years old, and my son was only 7 years old at that time. Plus, Richard was a lot younger than me. I was 31, and he was only 24 years old. However, I felt like I owed him an apology for what I did. I stood him up, so I give myself another chance to get to know him a little better. I am glad I decided to still be open to love and gave myself the chance to date him!

* * *

Richard has been a blessing for all four of us. His coming into our lives was not an easy one. I had to make some things clear to him, as well as really see if this life choice was going to work out. I made it clear to him that we are a package. He said he wasn't only in love with me, but also with the children. He said he'd never seen such well behaved and well mannered kids.

I warned him that if drinking and drugs were going to be in the mix, then he could pack his bags.

I told him that he could never hit any of my children. Since they were my children, I would discipline them myself in my own way. I was strict, but not abusive. Additionally, he was not allowed to shower my children with gifts and money. I was very cautious in case our relationship didn't work out since I never wanted my children to get hurt again. We agreed on all of those terms and more.

Richard has been the glory of my life for 25 years. He has been my soulmate and my best friend. He has stood by me all these years. He loves me so much that he would sacrifice his life for me and my three children.

This man has so much love to give to me and my children. Richard is a good kind man to my kids and to me. This year, Richard walked my youngest daughter down the aisle for her wedding. Richard has been a role model to all my children. While they were growing up, he was there for them for any activities that my children were involved in with school and sports. He would also help them with their homework. I remember when my oldest daughter would ask for his help in Algebra, he was always there to help her. When my son needed help to build a wooden car for Boy Scouts, Richard was there to show him how to carve the wood to make the car. He never makes any promises that he can't keep. We are blessed to have him in our lives.

As for my children, I am so blessed with them. They all have finished college and are successful in their lives. My eldest has a Ph. D. and my other two children are successful as well in their own lives. Throughout their childhood, I was always there for my three children. My mother never did care for me; I knew I would never do that to my children. They need me more than ever, like I needed my family by my side. So, I made a promise to my children that they came first.

Teddy, my children's biological father, passed away in 2004. For my two older kids who knew him as Dad, it was harder. My youngest child has no memory of him being around, unlike the older two who saw all the fighting and the broken promises.

All these years, I've made sure that Richard wouldn't make those same mistakes. I know I struggled a lot, but I kept my faith in God to take care of me and my children. My family has been a wonderful blessing to me; however, my journey and healing finally felt complete when I found yoga.

CHAPTER 14

The Healing Power of Yoga

"Yoga is the journey of the self, through the self, to the self."

- Bhagavad Gita

Yoga came into my life because I was having lots of pain from injuries since my early 30's. I had pain in my knees, neck, shoulders, and stomach. I met a director at a Y.M.C.A., and she said, "Why don't you try yoga? It's not that expensive."

I remember my first yoga class when I almost got kicked out by the instructor who told me to roll my mat and leave her class. I was laughing at myself throughout the whole class because I thought I looked funny having no flexibility whatsoever. The yoga poses were very difficult; I was locking my knees for a long time and struggled to get into the most basic poses. When I started, I didn't take it seriously and didn't really try to improve.

When I started, I didn't understand that yoga is about so much more than yoga pants and poses. It is about inner growth, understanding, and acceptance. Even on that first day, I knew yoga would lay an important role in my life.

When the instructor told me to leave the class, I said, "No!" in front of everybody. I knew I needed to stay and learn. I quickly started taking yoga very seriously. This was the beginning of many fruitful years of yoga. I become a yoga instructor and Thai yoga practitioner. I now have my own yoga studio.

* * *

One day in 2000, my very first yoga instructor at the Y.M.C.A., Bonnie, pulled me aside after class and wanted to talk to me. I thought I was in trouble again like on my very first yoga class. What she told me changed my life as this was the beginning of my career as a yoga instructor.

Bonnie told me that I had grown into my practice of yoga and that she'd like for me to consider getting some training to be a yoga instructor. I readily said yes as she assured me that my body was ready, even though deep inside, I didn't think I was ready.

Bonnie really inspired me. She believed in me. What would have happened if I didn't have that conversation with her way back then? She is the one who opened the door of opportunities for me. All I had to do was listen to her voice telling me it was time for me to go out and get some training.

What Bonnie said to me, "Your body is ready. Go get some training to be a yoga instructor," stuck in my head. It was two more years before I finally took the leap of taking my very teacher training in Dade County, Miami.

I received my first training from a spectacular, kind, and very helpful senior teacher, Ms. Bobbi Goldin. She practiced Iyengar Yoga, which is a technique that helps all people access the benefits of yoga. Ms. Goldin was very kind and helpful to all her students. She took her time and effort to let us understand the fundamentals and beauty of Yoga.1 "Regular practice of 'Iyengar Yoga' definitely integrates the body, mind and emotions."2 This Y.M.C.A. intensive training opened doors for me, and now I could teach my own classes.

In 2005, I took a year off of taking classes. I thought what I knew was good enough to teach yoga, but I was wrong. Six months later, I took another training in the Barkan Method of hot yoga in Fort Lauderdale, Florida.3 Jimmy Barkan is kind and wonderful to his students. He showed me that the beauty of the pose comes from the heart. Another ten days of immersion training helped me introduce this style to my students.

Finally, I opened my own yoga studio with the little money I got from Teddy's life insurance. From the $10,000, which was split between me and the kids, I had $1,800 to start the business. It was one of the best decisions I've ever made. Nelda's Yoga Studio has brought me and my community great joy. Through my yoga practice and instruction, I have been able to help others work through their physical and emotional challenges.

In 2006, I knew I needed more training. I came across Ana Forrest, and I knew right away her teachings were the ones for me.4 The training was for 27 days; quite a long training, but it was worth it. Her style gave me so much knowledge. It was designed to get rid of and let go of all the "junk" in my body. By "junk" I meant all the past abuses I went through and the effects of those, the anorexia and bulimia.

---

1   "Yoga Institute of Miami." *The*. Web. http://www.yogamiami.com/

2   "B K S Iyengar - Iyengar Yoga." *B K S Iyengar - Iyengar Yoga*. Web. http://bksiyengar. com/modules/IYoga/iyoga.htm

3   "Jimmy Barkan." *Barkan Method Hot Yoga*. Web. http://www.barkanmethod.com/

4   "STUDY WITH ANA." *Forrest Yoga with Ana Forrest*. Web. https://www.forrestyoga. com/

Additionally, I received training in Acroyoga Montréal. I'm so glad that I took the time to learn about a variety of yoga styles, philosophies, and practices. My training has greatly improved my own teaching and has given me wonderful opportunities to build connections and community.

> Acroyoga Montréal is about getting in where you fit in, creating a personal vocabulary in a cookie cutter world, and using the physicality of the practice to cultivate an original outlook. Nelda took our acroyoga teacher training in 2010 and quickly made her presence felt by all. She was the one all the other trainees went to for straight up advice, just the facts tempered with compassion, humour and wisdom. Some years later, it was our pleasure to be hosted by Nelda in Florida at her happening yoga emporium. Although we have trained hundreds of acroyoga instructors, Nelda captured and holds a special place in our heart.
>
> - Eugene Poku & Jessica Goldberg, founders of Acroyoga Montréal

After completing most of my yoga training and starting my own studio, I knew I needed additional training in similar healing practices that would enhance my yoga work. While I was in a training, I saw one of my fellow students giving a Thai yoga massage. I was fascinated to the beauty of the movement through yoga poses. When I got home from the training, I started searching for a Thai yoga massage school. I knew that it will benefit my studio to add this quality body work. I found an ashram, a Hindu retreat and community, about an 8 hours drive from my house that provided training in this unique massage.

After finishing a whole month of the training, I went home and started offering Thai massage to my students. They loved it, so I took another training from a different teacher in Mexico City for 10 days. Because of the positive response that I was receiving from my clients, I continued studying Thai yoga massage. I took another long training in Costa Rica where I received training in a different style of this massage. It has been very successful in my studio and the community loves it.

Although there have been many dark moments in my past, I have also experienced the kind support from strangers and loved ones throughout my journey. Yoga has given me a way to support others on their journey. I made a huge promise to myself that I would contribute my time to the people that needed my healing. I offer free services to my students who are in need. One student cannot drive herself to my studio, so I go to her home and provide my services free of charge.

Donna Pachota is one my students who experienced severe trauma on her head from falling down. As soon as she came home from the hospital, I offered her my services without accepting any payment.

> I have gone to Nelda's yoga classes for a few years. What has been most beneficial, though, has been the Thai massage she has done for me. I have suffered several episodes of sciatica and sacroiliac pain. I had sought help from several physicians for three years. I went to Nelda and after just a few treatments, it was gone.
>
> This past summer, I had a subarachnoid hemorrhage and blacked out. I have fully recovered, but during my recovery, I had a flare of the low back and leg pain. Nelda came to my house every day and gently did Thai

yoga on me, giving me the only relief I had in weeks. She didn't even accept payment. This was above and beyond anything I ever expected and it is something I will never forget.

- Donna Pachota, Nurse Practitioner

*   *   *

Yoga has made a huge impact on my life. It has helped me release all the sorrow from my childhood. It helps me talk about my life to my students. It has been a big ongoing therapy for me.

My yoga practice and meditation allow me to express my inner soul and also gives me a sense of direction in my life. I have learned not to pay attention to what people say about me. Before when people put me down, I worried a lot and it affected me so much. I know where I came from, and I will always remember to rise above all the struggles I had in my life.

I had to forgive myself and realize that I am no longer a victim. I learned, accepted, and forgave my two brothers and my mother for what they have done to me. I have a brand new life that began with my journey across the ocean.

As a mother of three wonderful children, this alone gave me the strength to conquer all of the memories of my painful past. My meditation allows me to be free. I have learned to stop hiding within myself. I have let go.

Some people say I am a hard teacher, but I learned to accept things without bitterness and cruelty inside me. I treat my students as students rather than friends. Some people find me hard core as a teacher/instructor, but I do care about my students. I know yoga is a tough and a very disciplined practice, so I hope my students will persevere and never give up on themselves in yoga or in their lives.

My breathing has taught me how to calm myself down. I only observe and breath at the same time. I know my practice of teaching yoga is only going to take me farther on my journey in life.

My yoga practice has really inspired me and allowed me to get past the obstacles in my life. Now I look back at myself, and I see the obstacles in my life have changed or shifted into spiritual ways or movements of my life. Before, I thought I could never go through them.

Yoga has taught me courage and strength. I am the same person, but a better one because I learned how to let go of many of the fears I had for so many years. I learned how to love myself more as a person. I learned how to embrace my past life and used that as a tool to be stronger. Now that I'm almost 56 years old, I feel more alive than ever.

I learned how to embrace the good and the bad. For example, if someone says I'm jealous about their success in life, I also embrace that moment because it is not about me, it is about them. It seems to me they are looking at their mistakes and blaming others for them. I know how I got here and built my foundation, which is filled with love and kindness.

When someone has hurt you verbally, you use that to strive for more. That's the case with me. I strive for more on the journey of my life. It propelled me to become more successful by taking years and years (and counting) of training and practice to become a yoga instructor and a teacher and to build my own business and yoga studio.

Yoga inspires me to be free at last. I know I will be doing this for as long as it takes me to keep unleashing my past sorrows. I thank all the people who have put me on the path of opportunities. In the past, people that I knew and trusted took advantage of my kindness, but I look at that as a learning experience that made me strive for more in my journey as a yoga teacher.

Conclusion

*"It's one of the greatest gifts you can give yourself,
to forgive. Forgive everybody."*

- Maya Angelou

I have stopped hiding and learned to let go of all my fears. I hope you can, too.

My story has released me from sorrow and helped me to realize to never give up on myself.
My story has made me stronger.
My story has allowed me to build a solid foundation of my life.

As for my mother, I still miss her. I will always love her, no matter what she had done to me.
As for my brothers, David and Jared, I wish them well and to be happy in life.
Will I forgive them? Yes, I already have. But will I forget the people who hurt me? The answer is no.

However, now I have another foundation that I need to keep building - My family, my children, my yoga practice! God gave me the opportunity to build and keep building a family that I dreamt of having, a yoga practice and my own students! These are blessings for me. I can make a difference in people's lives.

As a child, I always wanted a solid family; instead, I lived a life full of heartaches.

As a child, and even when I became an adult, I wanted to keep all my secrets, my life's painful past, but doing so only hurt me more and tore me apart.

My life has changed. My story has given me so much to look for in life.

My life has changed. The biggest reason for that are my children and their families.

I thought I didn't have the ability to change my life, I was helpless back then.

Now, it's different.

Never give up having faith in God.

Life is very precious.

It was never easy for me to raise three children, but I had to do what I had to do to survive and thrive. The choice was mine to build a solid foundation for my family.

Life can be very difficult, but with my faith and the conviction of never giving up no matter what, I hope I can inspire someone out there to do the same. I worked so hard to get to where I am today, in spite of all the odds.

What kept me and keeps me stronger are my children, their families, and of course, Richard. Our family continues to grow, and I now have a beautiful grandson.

My children believing in me as a yoga expert is incredible, but most of all, their believing in me as a mother is the most important thing for me. God has given me my life back. HE has gifted me more than I could ask for. Being a healer is a wonderful gift.

My journey is to continue doing great things with what he has given me. I believe in my heart that I have done what God has planned for me in my life. I still see so many things that my life has to offer in this world I'm living in.

I'm loving myself more everyday. I wake up every morning thanking God for giving me another day to live, laugh, care, and love. Life is a grand victory. I overcame that fear and painful past of my childhood. I want to continue to make a difference in people's lives.

If my story can inspire a mother who is struggling in life or a child who has been silent for many years because they are afraid to speak out, I hope to encourage her to never give up.

I am no longer afraid or ashamed of my childhood abuse or rape. I am only looking forward to a better life for me and my three children. God has given me the gift of life.

As for forgiveness, it is the key to the happiness I feel today. Do I forget the past? No, I don't, but I don't fear the past either. Letting go is an important part of what I have done to step up to a better level of my life.

Telling my story has made me stronger. My story has made me realize that I am no longer a victim of my own fear and shame. I came to realize that somehow I had to let go and forgive myself before I can forgive others who hurt me throughout my childhood. It has taken me along to time to let go and share my childhood abuse and rape without holding myself back in the past. Now, I can put everything behind me; all I have to do is look forward to the future that is waiting for me.

Acknowledgements

To the blessings that I have every single day of my life... my family!

To my three wonderful children, thank you for your unconditional love no matter what, for cheering me on in whatever I do, for teaching me patience and grace under pressure.

To the most precious apple of my eye, my dearest grandson, for showing me there's beauty and a sense of wonder all around us.

To my life partner, my rock, my best friend and soulmate, Richard, thank you for being a part of my life and that of my children's lives for the past twenty five years. You are a pillar of strength for us. You always showed me your important qualities that have guided me and gotten me through this journey called life.

To all my highly respected, world renowned teachers in the yoga and healing industry, who made such an impact in my life and my practice, thank you for believing in me, teaching me how to be strong, showing me how to let go of the fears of the past, letting me be me, and caring enough to provide me all the tools to succeed in business and in life. In gratitude...

> ... to Bobbi Goldin (BKS Senior Iyengar, Hatha Yoga) my very first teacher, who lead me to your fashion of BKS Iyengar style.

... to Jimmy Barkan - creator of The Barkan Hot Yoga Method

... to Ana T. Forrest - of Forrest Yoga Team

... to Tim Miller - of Ashtanga Yoga

... to Dr. Anthony James, author of *Ayurveda of Thailand* - SomaVeda Thai Yoga, thank you for teaching me the difference of stretching in Thai yoga. I still remember you making me do 20 times locating the lines of the legs. I am very grateful that you took the time to teach me what I needed to do in order to be more successful in this part of my Yoga practice. It is an experience of a lifetime to be able to say I was trained by one of the best teachers in the world.

... to Helman Itzhak - of Thai Yoga, thank you for your gift and caring to all your students. You taught us the beauty of Thai yoga.

... to Eugene and Jessica Poku - of Acroyoga

... to Tim Miller - of Ashtanga Yoga Center, thank you for believing in me as a yogi practitioner. Your fashion and the way you care for your students are so amazing. You always saw to it and made sure that we were safe in our practice, something that I carried along in my own practice...caring for my students.

To my students, who inspire me everyday to be the best I can be, thank you for the trust, support, and love you have given me all these years.

To my readers, who I hope will be inspired by this sixteen year project of a book that has freed me from sorrow and forwarded my life to healing.

To all those people that supported me and my vision, thank you for believing in me and making this book a reality. Thank you for being part of my healing process from a life of despair to seeing my story come alive through this book and thus inspiring and impacting people's lives.

To my wonderful book writing consultant and publisher, Susan Ordona of Social Buzz for Biz Publishing, for helping me get my sixteen years of writing my own story finally get to fruition in getting my message to the world in a very big way as a #1 International Bestselling Book and making me a #1 International Bestselling Author.

I would also like to thank Ms Carly Carruthers for her dedication and hard work as the editor of my book, *My Life, My Struggles, My Story*.

Thank you all from the bottom of my heart. Namaste.

About the Author

Nelda Barba is a well known Yoga teacher/instructor and a gifted healer. She is also the owner of Nelda's Yoga Studio, "Where Yoga is fun and healthy," a very popular yoga studio that offers different kinds of yoga class combinations of beach, private, and group sessions.

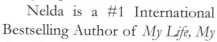

Nelda is a #1 International Bestselling Author of *My Life, My Struggles, My Story: A Transformational Journey from a Life of Childhood Abuse to a Life of Joy, Love and Success.*

Nelda has been teaching yoga since 2004 and has been inspired by the yoga traditions of BKS Iyengar, Hot Vinyasa, Ashtanga Vinyasa, Thai Yoga, Yin Yoga, AcroYoga, Viniyoga and many more. She studied with many world renowned yoga teachers.

With Nelda's expertise, healing gifts and the power of yoga, she has helped so many of her clients and students get back on their feet again, and lead more productive healthier lives.

A mother of three wonderful children and a doting grandma to her grandson, Nelda lives in Florida with her soulmate and life partner, Richard.

Learn more at **www.neldasyogastudio.com**

Get a copy of her book at
www.MyLifeMyStrugglesMyStoryBook.com

Made in the USA
Charleston, SC
25 January 2017